Nevada Ecoregions

- Northern Basin and Range
- Mojave Basin and Range
- Central Basin and Range
- Sierra Nevada

1. Sheldon National Wildlife Refuge
2. High Rock Resource Area
3. Anaho Island National Wildlife Refuge
4. Lahontan Valley Wetlands
5. Stillwater National Wildlife Refuge
6. Fernley Wildlife Management Area
7. Animal Ark
8. Damonte Ranch Wetlands
9. Verdi Community Library and Nature Center
10. Scripps Wildlife Management Area
11. Carson River Delta
12. Walker Lake
13. Alkali Lake WMA
14. Pilot Peak Wildlife Park
15. Ash Meadows National Wildlife Refuge
16. Clark County Wetlands Park
17. Moapa Valley National Wildlife Refuge
18. Pahranagat National Wildlife Refuge
19. Meadow Valley Wash
20. Wayne E Kirch Wildlife Management Area
21. Steptoe Valley Wildlife Management Area
22. Great Basin National Park
23. Ruby Lake National Wildlife Refuge
24. Franklin Lake Wildlife Management Area

Made in the USA

A POCKET NATURALIST® GUIDE

NEVADA WILDLIFE

A Folding Pocket Guide to Familiar Animals

T0124012

INSECTS & INVERTEBRATES

Black Widow Spider
Latrodectus mactans
To .5 in. (1.3 cm)
Has red hourglass marking on abdomen. Venomous.

Fiddleback Spider
Loxosceles reclusa
To .5 in. (1.5 cm)
Easily distinguished by violin-shaped marking on its back. Bites cause tissue degeneration.

Giant Desert Hairy Scorpion
Hadrurus arizonensis
To 5.5 in. (14 cm)

Black Saddlebags
Tramea lacerata
To 2.25 in. (5.2 cm)
Hindwings have large black patches at base. Black abdomen is yellow-spotted.

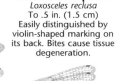

Vivid Dancer
Argia vivida
To 1.5 in. (4 cm)
Blue abdomen is marked by broad black rings and black triangles. Nevada's state insect.

Blue Dasher
Pachydiplax longipennis
To 2 in. (5 cm)
Perches horizontally with wings held downward.

Mormon Cricket
Anabrus simplex
To 2.5 in. (6 cm)

Yellow Jacket
Vespula pensylvanica
To .63 in. (1.6 cm)
Aggressive picnic pest can sting repeatedly.

Convergent Lady Beetle
Hippodamia convergens
To .5 in. (1.3 cm)

Large Carpenter Bee
Xylocopa spp.
To 1 in. (3 cm)
Large blue-black bee has a shiny abdomen.

Honey Bee
Apis mellifera
To .75 in. (2 cm)
Slender bee has pollen baskets on its rear legs. Can only sting once. The infamous killer bees are aggressive honey bees.

American Cockroach
Periplaneta americana
To 2 in. (5 cm)

Rhinocerous Beetle
Dynastes granti
To 2 in. (5 cm)
Largest U.S. beetle has two long horns forming a plier.

Water Strider
Gerris remigis
To .5 in. (1.3 cm)
'Skates' on the surface of quiet waters.

Whirligig Beetle
Family *Gyrinidae*
To .5 in. (1.3 cm)
Large swarms swirl around together on the water's surface.

Jerusalem Cricket
Stenopelmatus spp.
To 2 in. (5 cm)
Will bite.

BUTTERFLIES & MOTHS

Western Tiger Swallowtail
Papilio rutulus
To 4 in. (10 cm)

Pipevine Swallowtail
Battus philenor
To 3.5 in. (9 cm)

Cabbage White
Pieris rapae
To 2 in. (5 cm)
One of the most common butterflies.

Orange Sulphur
Colias eurytheme
To 2.5 in. (6 cm)
Note prominent forewing spot.

Western Tailed Blue
Cupido amyntula
To 1.25 in. (3.2 cm)
Note orange mark above tail on hindwings.

Red Admiral
Vanessa atalanta
To 2.5 in. (6 cm)

California Sister
Adelpha californica
To 3.5 in. (9 cm)

Mourning Cloak
Nymphalis antiopa
To 3.5 in. (9 cm)
Emerges early in spring.

Buckeye
Junonia coenia
To 2.5 in. (6 cm)

Monarch
Danaus plexippus
To 4 in. (10 cm)

Weidemeyer's Admiral
Limenitis weidemeyerii
To 3.5 in. (9 cm)

Bumblebee Moth
Hemaris diffinis
To 2 in. (5 cm)
Distinguished by clear wings and furry body.

Eyed Sphinx
Smerinthus cerisyi
To 3 in. (8 cm)

Underwing Moth
Catocala spp.
To 3.5 in. (9 cm)
Colorful hindwings are hidden when resting.

Mormon Metalmark
Apodemia mormo
To 1.25 in. (3.2 cm)

FISHES

Rainbow Trout
Oncorhynchus mykiss To 44 in. (1.1 m)
Note reddish side stripe.

Brown Trout
Salmo trutta To 40 in. (1 m)
Has red and black spots on its body.

Brook Trout
Salvelinus fontinalis To 28 in. (70 cm)
Reddish side spots have blue halos.

Lahontan Cutthroat Trout
Oncorhynchus clarkii henshawi
To 15 in. (38 cm)
Nevada's state fish.

Crappie
Pomoxis spp. To 16 in. (40 cm)

Largemouth Bass
Micropterus salmoides To 40 in. (1 m)
Note prominent side spots. Jaw joint extends past eye.

Bluegill
Lepomis macrochirus To 16 in. (40 cm)

Smallmouth Bass
Micropterus dolomieu To 27 in. (68 cm)
Jaw joint is beneath the eye.

Green Sunfish
Lepomis cyanellus To 12 in. (30 cm)

Channel Catfish
Ictalurus punctatus To 4 ft. (1.2 m)
Note adipose fin, black-spotted sides and rounded anal fin.

Common Carp
Cyprinus carpio To 30 in. (75 cm)
Introduced species.

Black Bullhead
Ameiurus melas To 2 ft. (60 cm)
Chin barbels are black.

Walleye
Sander vitreus To 40 in. (1 m)

Yellow Perch
Perca flavescens To 16 in. (40 cm)
Note 6-9 dark 'saddles' down its side.

REPTILES & AMPHIBIANS

Pacific Treefrog
Pseudacris regilla
To 2 in. (5 cm)
Color ranges from brown to green. Note dark eye stripe. Call is 2-part – kreck-ek – with the last syllable rising.

Northern Leopard Frog
Lithobates pipiens
To 4 in. (10 cm)
Brown to green frog has dark spots on its back. Call is a rattling snore with grunts and moans.

Great Basin Spadefoot Toad
Scaphiopus intermontanus
To 2 in. (5 cm)
Note vertical pupils.

Bullfrog
Lithobates catesbeianus
To 8 in. (20 cm)
Call is a deep-pitched – jug-o-rum.

Desert Tortoise
Gopherus agassizii To 15 in. (38 cm)
Domed shell has deep ridges. Nevada's state reptile.

Western Banded Gecko
Coleonyx variegatus To 6 in. (15 cm)

Western Fence Lizard
Sceloporus occidentalis To 9 in. (23 cm)
Has blue patches on its neck and belly.

Collared Lizard
Crotaphytus collaris To 14 in. (35 cm)
Note 2 dark collar markings.

Western Whiptail
Aspidoscelis tigris To 12 in. (30 cm)
Back and sides are dark-spotted. Note long tail.

Great Basin Gopher Snake
Pituophis catenifer deserticola
To 8 ft. (2.4 m)
Thick-bodied, barred snake.

Night Snake
Hypsiglena torquata To 2 ft. (60 cm)

Western Rattlesnake
Crotalus viridis
To 5 ft. (1.5 m)
Venomous snake has a spade-shaped head.

California Kingsnake
Lampropeltis getula californiae
To 7 ft. (2.1 m)
Dark snake has light crossbands on back.

Canada Goose
Branta canadensis
To 45 in. (1.14 m)

Western Grebe
Aechmophorus occidentalis
To 25 in. (63 cm)

American Coot
Fulica americana
To 16 in. (40 cm)

Northern Shoveler
Spatula clypeata   To 20 in. (50 cm)
Named for its large spatulate bill.

Mallard
Anas platyrhynchos To 28 in. (70 cm)

American Wigeon
Mareca americana To 23 in. (58 cm)

Northern Pintail
Anas acuta To 30 in. (75 cm)

Ring-necked Duck
Aythya collaris To 18 in. (45 cm)
Note white ring near bill tip.

Green-winged Teal
Anas crecca To 15 in. (38 cm)

Double-crested Cormorant
Phalacrocorax auritus
To 3 ft. (90 cm)

American White Pelican
Pelecanus erythrorhynchos
To 5 ft. (1.5 m)

Black-necked Stilt
Himantopus mexicanus
To 17 in. (43 cm)

Great Egret
Ardea alba
To 38 in. (95 cm)

Great Blue Heron
Ardea herodias
To 4.5 ft. (1.4 m)

Greater Roadrunner
Geococcyx californianus
To 2 ft. (60 cm)

Greater Sage-Grouse
Centrocercus urophasianus
To 30 in. (75 cm)

Mourning Dove
Zenaida macroura
To 13 in. (33 cm)
Call is a mournful –
ooah-woo-woo-woo.

Gambel's Quail
Callipepla gambelii
To 11 in. (28 cm)

Turkey Vulture
Cathartes aura
To 32 in. (80 cm)
Note two-toned underwings.

Great Horned Owl
Bubo virginianus
To 25 in. (63 cm)
Call is a resonant –
hoo-HOO-hoooo.

Rock Pigeon
Columba livia
To 13 in. (33 cm)

Downy Woodpecker
Dryobates pubescens
To 6 in. (15 cm)
The similar hairy woodpecker is larger and has a longer bill.

Northern Flicker
Colaptes auratus
To 13 in. (33 cm)
Wing and tail linings are red.

American Kestrel
Falco sparverius
To 12 in. (30 cm)

Golden Eagle
Aquila chrysaetos
To 40 in. (1 m)

Red-tailed Hawk
Buteo jamaicensis
To 25 in. (63 cm)

Northern Harrier
Circus hudsonius
To 22 in. (55 cm)
Note white rump.

Horned Lark
Eremophila alpestris
To 8 in. (20 cm)

Loggerhead Shrike
Lanius ludovicianus
To 9 in. (23 cm)

Northern Mockingbird
Mimus polyglottos
To 11 in. (28 cm)

Bushtit
Psaltriparus minimus
To 4 in. (10 cm)

Tree Swallow
Tachycineta bicolor
To 6 in. (15 cm)

Western Bluebird
Sialia mexicana
To 7 in. (18 cm)

American Robin
Turdus migratorius
To 11 in. (28 cm)

Red-breasted Nuthatch
Sitta canadensis
To 4.5 in. (11 cm)

Mountain Bluebird
Sialia currucoides
To 7 in. (18 cm)
Nevada's state bird.

American Crow
Corvus brachyrhynchos
To 22 in. (55 cm)
Call is a distinct – caw.

Western Meadowlark
Sturnella neglecta
To 9 in. (23 cm)

Common Raven
Corvus corax
To 27 in. (68 cm)
Call is a hoarse croak.

Mountain Chickadee
Poecile gambeli
To 6 in. (15 cm)

Black-chinned Hummingbird
Archilochus alexandri
To 3.5 in. (9 cm)

European Starling
Sturnus vulgaris
To 8 in. (20 cm)

Steller's Jay
Cyanocitta stelleri
To 14 in. (35 cm)

Woodhouse's Scrub-Jay
Aphelocoma woodhouseii
To 13 in. (33 cm)

Bohemian Waxwing
Bombycilla garrulus
To 8 in. (20 cm)
Red wing marks look like waxy droplets.

Black-billed Magpie
Pica hudsonia
To 22 in. (55 cm)

Great-tailed Grackle
Quiscalus mexicanus
To 18 in. (45 cm)
Long tail is keel-shaped.

White-crowned Sparrow
Zonotrichia leucophrys
To 8 in. (20 cm)

Bullock's Oriole
Icterus bullockii
To 8 in. (20 cm)

Red-winged Blackbird
Agelaius phoeniceus
To 9 in. (23 cm)

Dark-eyed Junco
Junco hyemalis
To 7 in. (18 cm)

Spotted Towhee
Pipilo maculatus
To 9 in. (23 cm)
Cheerful song is –
drink-your-tea or drink-tea.

House Sparrow
Passer domesticus
To 6 in. (15 cm)

Lesser Goldfinch
Spinus psaltria
To 4.5 in. (11 cm)

House Finch
Haemorhous mexicanus
To 6 in. (15 cm)

American Goldfinch
Spinus tristis
To 5 in. (13 cm)

Little Brown Bat
Myotis lucifugus
To 3.5 in. (9 cm)

Desert Cottontail
Sylvilagus audubonii
To 16 in. (40 cm)
Underside of tail is white.

Black-tailed Jackrabbit
Lepus californicus
To 25 in. (63 cm)
Tail and ears are black-tipped.

American Pika
Ochotona princeps
To 9 in. (23 cm)
Inhabits rock piles in mountainous areas.

Least Chipmunk
Neotamias minimus
To 9 in. (23 cm)
Note white stripes on side and face.

Golden-mantled Ground Squirrel
Callospermophilus lateralis
To 12 in. (30 cm)

White-tailed Ground Squirrel
Ammospermophilus leucurus
To 9 in. (23 cm.)

Yellow-bellied Marmot
Marmota flaviventris
To 28 in. (70 cm)

Western Spotted Skunk
Spilogale gracilis
To 19 in. (48 cm)

Common Porcupine
Erethizon dorsatum
To 3 ft. (90 cm)

Striped Skunk
Mephitis mephitis
To 32 in. (80 cm)

Long-tailed Weasel
Mustela frenata
To 21 in. (53 cm)

American Badger
Taxidea taxus
To 35 in. (88 cm)

American Beaver
Castor canadensis
To 4 ft. (1.2 m)

Common Gray Fox
Urocyon cinereoargenteus
To 3.5 ft. (1.1 m)

Common Raccoon
Procyon lotor
To 40 in. (1 m)

Kit Fox
Vulpes velox To 30 in. (75 cm)

Mountain Lion
Puma concolor
To 9 ft. (2.7 m)

Coyote
Canis latrans
To 52 in. (1.3 m)

Bobcat
Lynx rufus
To 4 ft. (1.2 m)

Pronghorn
Antilocapra americana
To 5 ft. (1.5 m)
Note 'pronged' horns.

Mule Deer
Odocoileus hemionus
To 7.5 ft. (2.3 m)
Rope-like tail is black-tipped.

Desert Bighorn Sheep
Ovis canadensis
To 6 ft. (1.8 m)
Nevada's state animal.

Black Bear
Ursus americanus
To 6 ft. (1.8 m)